# INTENTIONAL SOUL

# INTENTIONAL SOUL

*a collection of poetry and prose*

**Rya J. Hodges**

*Dedicated to my Heavenly Father*
I am truly the object of Your deepest love and af-
fection. You've allowed Christ's perfect love to
cast out fear, enabling me to be a intetnional lover
of You and others. Because of You, love is the
greatest aim in my life.

I am not claiming to be a great writer or poet, but an intentional observer of self.

Truthfully, I have been longing for balance to free me and spark a new calmness within me--it has been difficult. Sifting through the generational and societal layers that leave me feeling dejected and hidden. One day I woke up and realized I had been caged in the prison of perfection and misunderstanding. I needed a lot of strength to free myself. Owning my unique perspective of what it means to be human in this world. Laying a brick day by day, creating a safe haven for emotional and spiritual growth. Deep work is what I call it. The door to self-worth, vulnerability, and intention. I have greeted the inner parts of me that I suffocated with shame, finally giving them a voice without restraint. Allowing the fire of God to boil my shame to the surface, so the precious can be separated from the vile. Then letting Jesus kiss the scars and stitch the wounds. Those parts of me have begun to heal in the process of discovery. The harsh truth, staggering resolution, and tender risk have shown me the beauty in attending and befriending the issues I avoided with daily routines.

Sometimes, I worry that I won't find companions on this journey because I no longer choose to make a home out of ruptured perceptions. There is a subtle suspicion that being impartial will irritate those who aren't ready to be free. The judgment of self or others will not be my resting place. Perfection will not be a friend to me. Access to my spirit will not be granted. I am not a home for ignorance and fear to dwell in.

Writing this book has allowed me to see the creativity I bottled up. Wrestling with potential outcomes, I can't control. Nevertheless, I pray that if you're reading this, it's because you want to experience a different perspective. Not one of pain, hurt, or suffering. But one of gratitude, reflection, and intention. A view that prepares you for abundance and nudges you to be an observer of self.

*Eternity*

I am a mystery.
a simple explanation
won't reveal my truth.
every part of me
was woven with eternity.
a place unknown to natural history.

*Risk*

what good is love without God?
what good is compassion without grace?
what good is self-worth without reflection?
what good is vulnerability without risk?

*A love*

I was not created
for the comfort of people.
my heart was not designed
to experience shallow places
disguised as love.
the love created for me
never ends
never fades
and never forsakes.

*Unnatural*

I am more than
worthy of respect,
but it will not
come to a place
that has not made
a home amongst it.
respect without the self to come home to
is like the earth without water.

*Need*

I was everything standing in my way,
full of need, desire, and want
not realizing that
the way to fulfill my need
was to be grateful
for all I was.

*Forgive*

when I gave
myself an apology,
I forgot about
all the people
I claimed owed me one.

now, I owe me.

*Self*

go where it hurts.
go where you have
buried the truth.

let it breathe.
let it be.

please.
set the captive free.

*Everyone*

I wanted you to show me who I was
but you couldn't
I wanted you to save me
but you shouldn't
I wanted you to love me
but you wouldn't

then I found Him
and I tried to
hide my flaws
but I couldn't

*Salvation*

thoughts gone wrong
a heart gone mad
fear had to leave
because Your love
decided to stay

*Worldly knowledge*

I had to learn
how to let you go,
without losing
God in the process.

*Growth*

I welcomed
growth
like the sky
welcomes the sun

and just as
the sun adds life
growth did the same to my *strife*

*Choices*

I chose to attend my flaws
I chose to embrace them

I chose to befriend my wrongs
I chose not to chase them

I chose to face what no one else could
I chose to see a life that is good

*Before*

and I was worthy
before I knew it
was an option
not to be

worthy now
worthy then

worthy
shall I always be

*Urgent*

I had to value myself
more than
I desired the manifestation
of another's evaluation of me

I had to protect myself
more than
I wanted to be in the arms
of someone who wasn't me

I had to

*Times past*

there were times
there are times
when my shame
runs deeper than I can go

yet
I still find companionship
with my reflection
choosing to love
the one I see
fully & unconditionally

*Lies*

I have loved people
with lies
and they loved me back
with disregard

and still

I know that one day,
I shall love
with truth + consideration.

*Restart*

I need
the courage
to restart.

I need
faith
to rebuild.

I need
to let go
of the idea
that I am already
all that I will ever be.

*Redemption*

I chose
wrong
10 times

and
have been redeemed
11.

His love is a forever thing.

*No classroom*

who taught me
to unlove
the imperfect parts of myself
so subtly

to transform
my view of beauty
so drastically

*Human*

I believe in
vulnerability
the type that
is risky
and the type
that awakens

*6:33*

the heart that seeks the gifts,
does not understand
the value of
the Gift Giver.

now I know
my heart
should flow with love
as a river.

*Blinded*

quick to label
the one standing beside me,
ignoring my own inconsistencies.

*toxic. toxic. toxic.*

it is such an inner conflict
but the label looks so much better on you.

actually, I should take a walk in my own shoes.

*Version*

to every woman
who has been shamed
by perfection

truth is
you just have to stop
giving life
to the wrong version of you

*Heavy*

how am I still choosing you?

annulling thoughts
that are not my own
as if my personal preferences
are not good enough

these thoughts
have become baggage
to heavy to carry

I'm setting it down

*Fire*

give your *love* a life

to grow
to heal
to evolve

to usher in a refining light

*Gain*

reflecting upon myself
without ease

the question of growth
is not "where do I start"

but rather
what parts of me
do I first have to embrace?

no longer fearing the deception of loss
but gaining ground in my breakthrough

*Unity*

just because people relate to pain
doesn't mean you make a home with suffering

people often want to witness our frustration
spiraling out of control
accompanied by bad choices and shame

and then
there are those who want us
to enjoy the journey of untangling our frustrations
manifesting into wholeness

*Greenlight*

giving my flaws acceptance
has been reassuring

more peaceful
more relaxing

astounding & freeing

and then I realized
I had been
my own red light to growth

*Battlefield*

I had to choose to go into battle

a battle worth fighting
if I desired to taste freedom

I had to defeat my enemies
so I could finally stop hiding from them

now the battlefield of my mind
is ready for restructuring

*No*

your purpose to me has been cloudy
you became a symbol of rejection

sometimes a reminder
that what I desire
is not easily obtained
and most times
a threat to my ego

so, I never learned how to love you
like I've loved *yes*

even though *yes*
at times
has caused

the hushing of my alarmed spirit
the ignoring of my moral standard
& the intentional wounding of my self-worth

but now I am willing
to embrace you
and the glory to be revealed by your presence

*Comfort*

I use to chase after you
never wanting to be without the feeling you bring

but then I found a new companion -- growth
and though our times together
don't give me the feeling you do

I have been given this truth instead

a life worth building
can not include the both of you

I no longer have to chase
because growth has gladly taken your place

*Selfish*

your roots were hidden to me
but visible to Him

you acted as a mean of separation
from the only love
that could free me

oh, how I underestimated your nature

*Alone*

a journey only I can take

a path carved with risk
sometimes hopelessness
and a lot of stillness

*Mold*

what is the goal of life?

to impress people with lies
they can not decipher?
to cower amid opposition?
to prove I belong?

well,
the size of that box is wrong
I've been trying to fit in way too long.

*One more*

to finish
isn't the same as
to complete

I may have been finished with the past

but I had to
complete the lesson
to be free

remember the next step

*Cluttered*

some things I left undone
without a care
but definitely aware

entering a cycle
of struggle
pondering my despair

exposing the inadequacy
of the mental tools I had

but once I emptied
my toolkit

I could see clear space
and I was glad

*Difficult*

I am not always the sweetest
or kindest

but my capacity to love
will shatter mountains

disrupt hate
and defend the brokeness
in others

*What if*

what if this was done right
what if you thought of me when
the sun first shines bright

what if I would've found
the courage to say no
what if I would've decided
not to go

what if we gave it time

what if *this*
in fact
isn't even divine

*Pieces*

I've fallen into many pieces
scattered amongst men

who chose to see
what I lacked
with no intention
of helping me gain it back

*Anyhow*

all of me wants
to hide and fall into
Your arms

giving in to the calling
of Your heart

all of me wants
to show up and stand
for Your Ways

giving in to the
Great Commission
of this present day

*Be*

I look for new ways
to calm the war inside of me

to become everything that
looks like love

unaware that what I seek
is the act of being

and through seeing
the world through
Your eyes

I can be a
representative of
love in action

*Wyd*

late night texts
to fuel my ego

while my spirit is saying
"suffer it"
"please don't choose this"

sending replies not meant
for many eyes

wrestling with innocence
and my state of demise

knowing I shouldn't
but yearning for the
element of surprise

but I hear You
I think I'll just close my eyes

*Home*

there's no need to look
in unfamiliar places

this journey ahead
has been predestined

reflection, progression, and change
will always lead you back home
safe

*The Grind*

diploma.
degree.
job.

marriage.
wife.
child.

retire.
travel.
expire.

why is this the formula of a life
to be admired?

*Away*

I can hardly see the value
others cling to

blinded by my own insecurities
and brusque judgment

being too aware of the
flaws I wear in private

traveling in the opposite direction
of other people's sincere embrace

*Permission*

I am allowed to
love myself
gently
by tapping into
my divine resources
attently

*Together*

the quest isn't about
creating who I want to be
when you're standing beside me

but rather
who am I without you?

*Misunderstood*

I've had people take away
their interest
because of a battle I had to fight through

it rendered insufficient funds
from the bank of their love

I was left alone
and judged unjustly

but today I stand
tall, secure, and confident
so robustly

*Life lessons*

I use to think
education was constricted
to a classroom,
but no matter
how much knowledge I gained,
it just wasn't enough to keep me sane

so I changed the location
of my learning

ran to God
and filled my mind
with life, sacrifice, and discerning

*Match*

If I gave a lot
I often knew
it wouldn't be matched

and that was okay
because the intent of
my heart was pure

even though the intent
of others can be obscure

I held on to the truth
that the reward of a transparent heart is sure

*Flaws can write*

I had to stop taking myself
so seriously
because there was no joy in that

my flaws write a beautiful story
and I no longer
want to run from that

*Clingy*

cling to your healing
for the sake of having yourself

cling to your growth
for the sake of your mental health

*Incomplete adult*

what's worse
aging but not maturing?
changing but not progressing?
growing but not manifesting?
letting go but not healing?
hearing but not doing?
moving but not advancing?

at some point you
must decide to turn the dial
and channel the fullness
of this life

*Handled*

there has been
considerations
fears
and roadblocks

but I prepared myself
to handle them

no longer could I sit back
allowing them to handle me

*Perspective*

instead of seeing if
the glass is half full
or half empty

I decided to be the water

*Leaving*

staying frozen in pain
because someone else can relate

is not ideal
and I don't like the way it feels

this strain
has come to an end

so I'm removing the blocks
that has covered the path
I must journey
to amend

*All is well*

I chose you
and at the time
it was the best I knew to do

but instead of being mad
at how the situation turned out

I'm glad I had the courage to
love without doubt

*No chance*

who I was becoming
never had a chance
because you let your idea
of who I should've already been
rule out who I am

*Breakthrough*

I have to give myself permission
to do things that other people
don't know how to do.

why did I wait for someone else
to grant me access
to the parts of me
that was reserved
for me to travel

had I waited on them to
embrace awareness before
I was able to find my own

I would've waited a lifetime
with a heart full of stone

*Harsh*

to the woman
who desires love from a man

first deal with
your own issues

you have bottled up sorrows
that needs your growth to be tissues

avoiding your truth can push a man away
tune in though and don't
let your self-worth go astray

a man can not define your worth
and he's not obligated to just
deal with your mess

become a woman who is whole
and can relieve him from more stress

*This love*

I use to think this love
was about the benefits
I didn't know this love
was about selflessness

I use to think this love
was about making requests

I didn't know this love
was meant to deal with
matters of the heart
that needed to be addressed

I use to think this love
was about partnership

I didn't know this love
Was created solely for fellowship

I use to think
but I really didn't know

now I do
and it's all thanks to You

*The process*

It isn't a sugar-coated cradle
it presses on your aches
it feels like being thirsty in a hot dessert
& it looks like your home covered in white fog

but nothing worth revealing
happens without the transformation
it brings

*JOMO*

everyone speaks of the fear of missing out
but there is joy in missing out

the joy of missing out on
self-sabotage
compromised standards
filtered love
comparison

there's joy in focusing on your growth
because there is much to gain
like missing out on
sustained pain

*I loved you*

I use to blame you for the pain I felt
but I had to mature and take responsibility
for my own decisions

I decided to ignore the signs
I decided to quiet my concerns

and I fooled myself into believing

that just because I was a different woman
from the rest
that you somehow were a different man
without your learned patterns and mess

*Don't overlook*

I don't have to be like anyone else
and though I encourage being my
authentic self

that does not excuse me from dealing
with my own inconsistencies
triggers
fears
biases
perceptions
judgments
and a sense of attitude correctness

my love for self doesn't have to include
a tolerance for my growth blockers

*Rejection*

listening to her speak
sitting quietly
never making a peep

but one day I dared to ask

"why are you here?"
and she responded

"because you keep opening the door for me
I happen to catch you
right before you leave
your home of comfort

you entertain me,
considering my every word

but if you decided
not to open up for me
eventually, I'd stop showing up
and look for someone else to entertain me"

*Condition*

pour love,
love,
and more love
over the healing scars of your heart

nurture,
nurture,
nurture
so you're healing doesn't fall apart

*Understanding*

why are we so quick
to call ourselves fools
for choosing to love

even if our hearts collide
with carelessness

it is foolish to not
choose love
no matter how much
we think our reasoning
makes sense

*Us*

I am.
you are.
we are.

art. multifaceted. eternal beings.

we can't let baneful standards
destroy the divine traces of our image
with blurred lines filled with the ink of hate.

*Primary*

we are a reflection
of how we treat ourselves.

a reflection of how
a man treats us
isn't the primary manifestation
of our worth,

but rather
the secondary image
of what we first mirrored
for ourselves.

*Gaze*

I look at myself
like a mother looks at
her newborn child

in awe

*Farther*

being observant of myself
took me further
than observing others
ever did

*Be careful*

stop repressing
stop stressing

let it be
let it go

avoidance is the
first step in self-denial

*Hired by self*

we must remind ourselves
of our existence

it is not
anyone else's job

*Responsible*

the effects of neglect
& the pain of abuse
is not my fault

but the responsibility
of healing is mine

*Last time*

when was the last time
I told myself, "I love you because..."

when was the last time
I made myself a promise

when was the last time
I told myself, "I forgive you for…"

*Slow down*

never be too be busy
with life's demands,

that you allow your
wellness to wither
away with the days.

*Her favorite*

fear comes in many forms
and control is her favorite.

*Persuaded*

I had to learn
how to be
sure of myself,
so I could identify
when someone else's love
was sure of me too.

*Stay with me*

solitude taught me
how to feel the emotions
I avoided with other people's company.

*Church*

I am grateful for
every tear that fell from my eyes
every gesture of lifted hands
every resounding roar of victory

I am thankful for
every knee-buckling praise
every fear shattering truth
every sweet sound of worship

*Show up*

create space for expression,
whatever it is.

make it sacred.
make it profound.

the world needs to
hear a new sound.

*Evaluation*

how are you showing
up for your life?

if it is anything less
than how you are showing
up for others

it is time to re-evaluate

*Unpacking*

I was unintentionally carrying:
self-criticism
mental trauma
blame of others
distorted views of love

I ignored my messy junk drawers
for a long time
then I finally
decided to clean it out

and I intentionally discovered:
self-compassion
vulnerability
forgiveness
&
a new method of love

*Ego-free*

the ego convinced me
that asking for help
was a sign of weakness

but strength confirmed
that being in need
is the glory of being human

it is an opportunity to
stand in vulnerability
allowing someone else
to be the hero
without shame

*They lied*

your pain doesn't have to be
your identity

it's okay to let wholeness
paint a new picture

*Residence*

who knew loving myself
would hurt sometimes

who knew that the perceptions
of others would block my
compassion for self

who knew the only reason
it hurt so bad
was because I let society
determine what deserves love

now I decide
and love of self is where
I shall reside

*Leaving it behind*

no longer will I
overextend my presence
to motives unknown
that leave my heart
torn

*Admiration*

the bravery to bring
attention to my own struggles
is a humble gesture inspired
by the liberation of others.

*Choose*

happiness is not some far off
idea that is hard to comprehend.

happiness is a choice
you make from within

*Kingdom wealth*

my blessings exceed
any material possession
because my heart and mind
are growing into a
higher expression.

things can be taken away without question
but who I've become in this process
will never fade in a recession.

*Continuously*

In all that you do,
be present,
be aware,
be fair.

From my soul to your soul--thank you.

connect with Rya J. Hodges
instagram: @ryajhodges
website: www.ryahodges.com
email:ryajhodges@gmail.com